LOSOP
Momentum
STAFFROOM EDITION

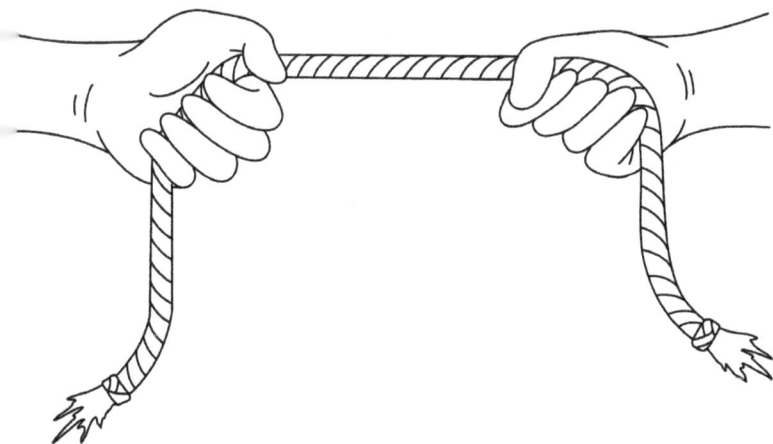

For information about school wide professional development, team training or individual coaching in the application of Loving our Students on Purpose please contact:

- www.godwinconsulting.com.au
- admin@godwinconsulting.com.au

Editor: Allison Slack
Cover Design by Ashley Beck
Interior Design and Layout by Daniel
ISBN: 978-0-6459046-1-1 (pbk)
ISBN: 978-0-6459046-2-8 (ebk)

TABLE OF CONTENTS

INTRODUCTION:

REFRESHING OUR CONNECTION THROUGH LoSoP

Welcome to this collection of 10-minute staff meeting refreshers designed to bring the principles of Loving Our Students On Purpose (LoSoP) into focus in your daily work. As educators, our goal is not just to teach academic content but to build meaningful, lasting connections with our students and colleagues. The heart of LoSoP is the belief that true transformation happens when we prioritise connection, respect, and responsibility in every interaction.

These 40 refreshers are intended to be used in staff meetings to remind and recalibrate us to the core values that make LoSoP such a powerful approach to education. Each session is designed to spark discussion, personal reflection, and practical application. Through brief teaching summaries, creative metaphors, and thought-provoking questions, this book will guide you and your team in maintaining a culture of love, trust, and connection in your school.

As you engage with these sessions, you'll revisit foundational LoSoP principles like empathy, responsibility, and trust. You'll reflect on your personal experiences, share insights with your colleagues, and discover new ways to apply these concepts in your classroom or leadership. The goal is not just to teach these principles, but to live them—to let them shape how we approach every relationship in our professional lives.

Whether you're leading the discussion or participating in small groups, these refreshers will serve as a quick yet powerful way to reconnect with what matters most: creating a school environment where every student and staff member feels valued, empowered, and connected. Let these sessions be a reminder that love is a choice, connection is a goal, and we are all responsible for cultivating a space where learning and growth can thrive.

'Thank you for creating such a beneficial program for educators.'
– Monica Lemke, USA

'Exceeded my expectations.' – Connie Jakab, Canada

'Loving Our Students On Purpose has given us a framework and language to begin transforming our school culture.' – Ed QLD, Australia

'Our teachers were delighted.' – Matthew Gilbank, Australia

A NOTE FROM BERNII

Dear Educators,

Thank you for taking the time to dive into Loving Our Students On Purpose (LoSoP) through these 10-minute refreshers. I created this resource to help you reconnect with the heart of what we do every day—building meaningful relationships with the students and colleagues around us. In the busyness of school life, it's easy to get caught up in the tasks and challenges, but at the core of it all is the power of connection.

This book is designed to serve as a quick but powerful reminder of the principles that guide our work. I hope these sessions inspire you to reflect, share, and take intentional steps to strengthen the bonds you create with those in your care. Each session offers a new opportunity to pause, recalibrate, and remember why connection is so crucial in education.

I believe in the potential each of you holds to create lasting impact through love, trust, and responsibility. Thank you for being part of this journey and for your dedication to nurturing students with care and purpose. Together, we are shaping not just classrooms but our future nation, and it all starts with connection.

Warm regards,

Bernii Godwin

INSTRUCTIONS FOR LEADING THE LoSoP MOMENTUM SESSION

Welcome to your role as the facilitator for this LoSoP Momentum session! This guide is designed to help you lead an engaging, thought-provoking session with your team. While the material provides a structured outline, it's important to make this session your own. The stories, metaphors, and questions provided are here as guidelines, but we encourage you to personalise the content with your own experiences, creativity, and style.

Here's how to get the most out of this session:

1. **Make It Personal:**
   The most impactful stories are often the ones that come from your own life. As you prepare to lead the session, think about moments in your own classroom or leadership journey that align with the principles of LoSoP. Sharing these personal stories will make the session more relatable and authentic for your audience.

2. **Get Creative with Metaphors:**

   While this guide provides metaphors like losing phone connection or sailing with a rudder, feel free to adapt or swap in your own metaphors that resonate with you. Whether it's something from your daily life or an experience that left an impression, your unique take will add depth and engagement.

3. **Adjust the Timing:**

   This session is flexible, so you can tailor it to the time available. If you're using it as a quick 10-minute refresher, focus on the key teaching points and one or two discussion questions. If you're leading a longer staff workshop (20 or 30 minutes), take the time to dive deeper into the material, share more stories, and allow for richer discussions. Adapt the depth of the session based on how much time you have with your group.

4. **Encourage Participation:**

   The goal of this session is to create dialogue and reflection. While you'll be leading, invite others to share their own stories, reflections, and insights. Encourage creative thinking and make space for people to express their thoughts. Remember, it's about building a collective understanding of the power of connection.

5. **Apply the Lessons to Your Context:**

   Every classroom and team is different, so take the core LoSoP principles and tailor them to fit the unique dynamics of your group. If a particular metaphor or story doesn't quite align with your setting, swap it out for something that does. What matters is that the principles—connection, empathy, responsibility—shine through.

6. **Keep It Interactive:**

    Use the reflection and discussion questions provided as springboards for conversations, but don't hesitate to adapt them. Invite group discussions, partner sharing, or personal reflection, depending on what feels most natural for your audience. Encourage the group to engage deeply with the material and apply it to their daily work.

Most importantly, have fun with this! The heart of LoSoP is about creating genuine, meaningful connections, and that begins with how you lead this session. Be creative, be vulnerable, and lead by example. Your unique perspective will make this session a valuable and memorable experience for everyone involved.

WEEK 1:

THE LoSoP PHILOSOPHY

Love means doing what is best for someone with respect, honour, and care.

The Loving Our Students On Purpose (LoSoP) philosophy is rooted in the belief that love means doing what is best for someone with respect, honour, and care. This approach shifts the focus away from control and fear-based methods to fostering healthy, connected relationships. Love, in this context, becomes a deliberate choice, guiding interactions between educators and students, and helping create environments where connection thrives. The four key principles of LoSoP Philosophy are:

1. Our goal is connection.
2. Love is a powerful choice.
3. Fear is the enemy of connection.
4. Building and protecting connection is a learning journey.

Picture This:

Imagine a sailing boat on the open sea. The winds represent the challenges and emotions we face daily, which can push us off course. The LoSoP philosophy is like the rudder, guiding the boat toward its destination—connection. Without the rudder, the boat drifts aimlessly, at the mercy of the wind. But with careful steering, the rudder keeps the boat on course, navigating through both calm and stormy waters. In relationships, love and connection are the rudder, ensuring we stay intentional and purposeful, no matter the circumstances.

Let's Make It Real:

In small groups, share a personal story of when you saw the power of connection in your own classroom or leadership. This could be an example of when you moved away from control-based methods and embraced connection, and how it transformed your relationship with students or staff.

Discussion Questions:

1. Can you think of a time when you felt connected to a student or colleague in a meaningful way? What did you do to foster that connection?
2. How do you see fear affecting relationships in your current school environment, and what steps can you take to replace fear with love and connection?
3. What small changes can you make in your daily interactions to prioritise connection over control?

Action Goal:

Practice intentional acts of love and connection each day by checking in with at least one student or colleague to strengthen your relationship.

In the LoSoP philosophy, love means doing what is best for someone because we respect, honor, and care for them. Love is not about getting something from someone, but about giving. It is fundamentally others-focused rather than self-focused--it puts "we" before "me."

LoSoP Pg 25

WEEK 2:

CONNECTION AS THE GOAL

Make connection the priority in all interaction.

In LoSoP, the primary aim in every relationship—whether between students, teachers, or colleagues—is connection. Disconnection is never an option, and when it does occur, it's essential to restore it with clear boundaries and a commitment to trust. Making connection the goal means prioritising understanding and empathy over punishment, ensuring that each person feels valued and heard. This principle shapes a connected classroom culture where students thrive emotionally, socially, and academically.

Picture This:

Think about a time when you've been on an important phone call and suddenly lost signal. The conversation abruptly cuts off, and until you regain connection, nothing can move forward. In relationships, disconnection works the same way—when we lose connection, progress stops. Just like you work to move to a better location to regain signal, in relationships, we must also be intentional about restoring connection, ensuring we are heard and understood.

Let's Make It Real:

In partners, reflect on a time when connection wasn't the goal in your relationship with a student or colleague. What was the outcome? How could shifting the goal to connection have changed the situation?

Discussion Questions:

1. What challenges do you face when making connection the goal with students, especially those who are difficult to reach?
2. Can you identify moments where you may have prioritised behaviour management over connection? How could you approach these situations differently?
3. What steps can you take to ensure that connection remains the primary goal in your daily interactions with students or colleagues?

Action Goal:

Set a daily reminder to prioritise connection over control in every interaction, focusing on building trust.

Teaching students to be powerful, responsible, and internally motivated toward love and connection begins with becoming those things yourself. Your example of self-control and pursuing the goal of connection, more than your words, is what will lead and invite students to imitate you.

LoSoP Pg 27

WEEK 3:

THE POWER OF CHOICE

Love is a powerful, intentional choice.

As educators, we entered this profession because we chose to make a difference. We chose to study, to work in this field, and to step into classrooms. Yet, our students didn't choose us—they didn't choose who would guide them each day. But every day, we have the opportunity to continue choosing them. It would be wonderful if this choice came effortlessly, but the truth is, we must intentionally choose connection each day. By making the deliberate choice to connect with our students, we invite them to reciprocate and choose us in return, creating a bond built on freedom and mutual respect.

Picture This:

Imagine you're standing at a crossroads each morning. One path leads you toward connection, the other toward disengagement. Every day, you stand at that crossroad and make a decision. By choosing the path of connection, you open the possibility for your students to walk with you down that same path. Just as you choose them, you give them the freedom to choose you. The beauty of this choice is that it builds trust, connection, and the kind of relationships that create positive change.

Let's Make It Real:

Share a personal story about a time you had to make the intentional choice to connect with a student, despite challenges. How did this choice impact the relationship, and how did it open the door for the student to choose connection in return?

Discussion Questions:

1. How do you feel about the idea that we choose our students, and they can choose us in return?
2. Can you recall a time when you had to make an active choice to connect with a student? How did that choice influence the relationship?
3. What can you do to create opportunities for students to choose connection with you in return?

Action Goal:

Give your students a chance to make choices that involve you today— whether it's how they approach a task, or the freedom to express their thoughts. Let them see that you choose them, and they have the freedom to choose you in return.

This kind of powerful choice is something we will only be able to make consistently through cultivating a high sense of personal freedom, responsibility, and agency. This is what moves us to be internally motivated and focus on controlling and managing ourselves and our choices first and foremost.

LoSoP Pg 27

WEEK 4:

FEAR IS THE ENEMY OF CONNECTION

Understand how fear undermines connection.

Fear is a powerful emotion that can easily undermine relationships and create barriers to genuine connection. In the classroom, fear-based strategies—whether through control, punishment, or intimidation—may produce compliance but do not foster trust or a healthy learning environment. In LoSoP, we recognise that fear is the enemy of connection, and removing it from our interactions allows us to build stronger, more trusting relationships.

Picture This:

Imagine trying to hold onto a delicate butterfly. If you grasp it too tightly out of fear that it will fly away, you end up harming it. But if you hold it gently and allow it the freedom to move, it may stay with you willingly. Fear works in much the same way. When we operate out of fear, we try to control outcomes, and in doing so, we damage the connection. Releasing fear allows us to trust the process and foster meaningful relationships.

Let's Make It Real:

In small groups, discuss a time when fear impacted your ability to connect with a student or colleague. How did fear affect your actions, and what was the result? What could have been done differently to remove fear from the situation?

Discussion Questions:

1. Where do you see fear affecting your relationships with students or colleagues?
2. What can you do to remove fear from your interactions and replace it with trust and connection?
3. How can you create an environment that encourages freedom and connection rather than compliance through fear?

Action Goal:

Identify one area where fear might be affecting a relationship and take a step to remove it by using empathy and understanding instead.

> *The goal of self-preservation is the exact opposite to the goal of love and connection; it puts "me" before "we" and moves us away from others rather than toward them.*

LoSoP Pg 28

WEEK 5:

BUILDING AND PROTECTING CONNECTION IS A LEARNING JOURNEY

Connection requires continuous learning, growth, and adjustment.

Building and maintaining strong connections in the classroom or workplace is not a one-time event; it's a continuous process of learning, growth, and adjustment. In LoSoP, we recognise that building connection takes time, and protecting it requires ongoing effort. Mistakes will be made, but the commitment to connection allows for grace, restoration, and deeper understanding as we journey through the process.

Picture This:

Imagine teaching a child to walk. When they stumble and fall, you don't assume they'll never learn. You don't yell or give up. Instead, you steady them, offer encouragement, and cheer them on as they try again. The process is filled with falls and missteps, but with each attempt, they grow stronger and more confident. Building connection works the same way—it requires patience, support, and continuous effort. Even when mistakes happen, the key is to keep going, offering guidance and encouragement along the way.

Let's Make It Real:

As the presenter, share a personal story about a time when building or protecting connection was challenging, either with a student or colleague. What did you learn from that experience, and how did you continue to strengthen the connection over time?

Discussion Questions:

1. How do you view the process of building and protecting connection in your classroom or workplace?
2. What challenges have you faced in maintaining connection, and how did you overcome them?
3. What practices can you implement to continually protect and nurture connection in your daily interactions?

Action Goal:

Reflect on one challenging relationship and commit to taking one positive action toward rebuilding or strengthening that connection.

The Loving Our Students on Purpose philosophy affirms that our primary goal is not simply that students learn to stop problematic behaviors. Ultimately, we want them to learn to love.

LoSoP Pg 29

WEEK 6:

THE LoSoP COMMITMENT

Remove fear, show vulnerability, and establish core commitments.

The LoSoP commitment is a three-step process that encourages educators to remove fear from their interactions, show vulnerability in building connections, and establish core commitments that foster a connected culture. These steps are essential to creating an environment where both students and staff feel safe, valued, and connected.

1. **Stop showing the 'Yellow Truck'** – Remove fear from your toolkit.
2. **Start showing your heart** – You are half of this connection.
3. **Establish core commitments** – Build a culture where connection is the foundation.

Picture This:

Imagine the Yellow Truck—big, powerful, and intimidating. It's tempting to drive it through difficult situations, pushing others into submission or compliance. But while the Yellow Truck may get things moving temporarily, it leaves people feeling small and disconnected. Real connection is built not by driving over others but by stepping out of the truck, showing your heart, and creating space for understanding and respect.

Let's Make It Real:

In partners, reflect on a time when you showed vulnerability or made a commitment to build connection in your classroom or workplace. What was the impact, and how did it shape your relationship with the other person?

Discussion Questions:

1. How does showing vulnerability strengthen your connections with students or colleagues?
2. What are some specific ways you can remove fear from your interactions to build a more connected environment?
3. How can the LoSoP commitments guide your daily interactions in creating a connected classroom or workplace culture?

Action Goal:

Practice vulnerability by sharing your heart in a conversation where you might typically remain guarded.

We must cultivate a mindset that says, I do not control you. On a good day, I control me. That's where my focus is. No matter what you do, or what your learning process is today, I am going to control me. My love is going to stay on towards you.

LoSoP Pg 32

WEEK 7:

RESTORING CONNECTION

Restore connection through intentional actions and clear boundaries.

Disconnection can happen in any relationship, whether it's between teachers and students or among colleagues. In LoSoP, we emphasise that disconnection is not the end but an opportunity for restoration. When trust is broken, clear boundaries and intentional actions can help restore the connection, rebuilding the relationship with even greater strength. Restoring connection involves acknowledging where things went wrong, taking responsibility, and working together to re-establish trust.

Picture This:

Imagine two people holding onto a rope that represents their connection. When the relationship is strong, that rope is made of durable, thick material. But when disconnection happens, the rope weakens, as if it's now made of tissue paper—fragile and easy to tear. Restoring connection is like weaving the rope back together, one strand at a time, making it stronger than it was before. It requires time, care, and commitment, but in the end, the rope becomes durable once again.

Let's Make It Real:

In small groups, discuss a time when disconnection happened in a relationship with a student or colleague. How did you go about restoring that connection, and what impact did the restoration process have on the relationship?

Discussion Questions:

1. What steps can you take to restore connection when it is broken in your relationships with students or colleagues?
2. How do boundaries help in the process of restoring trust and connection?
3. How does restoring a broken connection contribute to a stronger, more resilient relationship in the long term?

Action Goal:

Reach out to someone with whom you have lost connection and take a small step toward restoring the relationship.

If you let go of the goal of connection, there is nothing a student can do to connect with you. Only you are responsible for your half of the connection.

LoSoP Pg 129

WEEK 8:

THE ROLE OF BOUNDARIES IN CONNECTION

Boundaries protect both individuals and relationships.

Boundaries are essential to creating safe and healthy relationships. In LoSoP, we teach that boundaries protect both the individual and the relationship, ensuring that respect and care remain at the forefront of all interactions. Boundaries are not about control but about establishing clear expectations that allow for trust and connection to flourish. When boundaries are clear and respected, connection becomes safer and more sustainable.

Picture This:

Imagine a river flowing through a valley. Without the riverbanks, the water would spread uncontrollably and become a flood. The riverbanks, or boundaries, help guide the water safely on its course. In relationships, boundaries act as those riverbanks, keeping the flow of connection steady and protecting the integrity of the relationship.

Let's Make It Real:

As the presenter, share a time when you set clear boundaries in a relationship with a student or colleague. How did those boundaries help protect and strengthen the connection?

Discussion Questions:

1. How do boundaries create safety in your relationships with students or colleagues?
2. Can you think of a time when unclear boundaries led to disconnection? What could have been done differently?
3. What steps can you take to establish and maintain healthy boundaries that protect connection in your classroom or workplace?

Action Goal:

Set or reinforce a boundary in a relationship that needs it, ensuring it supports connection rather than control.

> *When disconnection occurs and trust is broken, clear boundaries will make it safe for connection to be restored.*

LoSoP Pg 34

WEEK 9:

CELEBRATING SUCCESS

Acknowledging achievements reinforces connection.

In LoSoP, celebrating success is a powerful way to reinforce connection and build a positive culture in the classroom or workplace. No matter how small, every achievement should be acknowledged, as it sends the message that each person is valued, chosen, and appreciated. Celebrating success shifts the focus from problems and challenges to growth and progress, fostering an environment where individuals feel encouraged and motivated to continue developing.

Picture This:

Imagine a marathon runner nearing the finish line. Every cheer from the crowd energises them, giving them the strength to push through the final stretch. In the same way, celebrating small successes with students or colleagues boosts morale and helps them move forward with confidence and determination.

Let's Make It Real:

In small groups, reflect on a recent success—either personal or professional—that you celebrated or failed to acknowledge. How did that celebration (or lack thereof) impact your connection with others? How could you bring more intentional celebration into your daily routine?

Discussion Questions:

1. How does celebrating small successes impact the overall culture of your classroom or workplace?
2. Can you think of a time when celebrating a success strengthened your connection with a student or colleague?
3. What are some specific ways you can incorporate more celebration into your daily interactions to reinforce connection?

Action Goal:

Identify one small success in a student's or colleague's work this week and publicly celebrate it to reinforce positive behaviour.

We will celebrate every success, no matter the size, and will always seek to send the message to each person that they are valued, known, and worthy.

LoSoP Pg 34

WEEK 10:

TRUST AND TRANSPARENCY

Transparency fosters trust and stronger relationships.

Trust is the foundation of all meaningful relationships, and transparency is one of the keys to building that trust. In LoSoP, we recognise that when we are open and honest with students and colleagues about what is going on inside, it creates a safe space for connection. Trust allows relationships to flourish, and transparency helps prevent misunderstandings and fosters a deeper sense of mutual respect.

Picture This:

Think of trust like a glass window. When the glass is clear, you can see through it and understand what's on the other side. But if the glass becomes foggy or covered in dirt, it becomes difficult to see, and you might misinterpret what's happening. Transparency helps keep the window clean, allowing for clear and honest communication.

Let's Make It Real:

Reflect quietly on a time when transparency helped you build or restore trust in a relationship with a student or colleague. How did being open and honest affect the connection? What could you have done differently to strengthen that trust?

Discussion Questions:

1. How does transparency affect your ability to build trust in relationships?
2. Can you think of a time when a lack of transparency led to disconnection or misunderstanding? How was it resolved?
3. What steps can you take to ensure that transparency is a core part of your interactions with students or colleagues?

Action Goal:

Have an open and transparent conversation with a student or colleague about a challenge you're facing and ask for their input.

We will always demonstrate trust in this relationship by being transparent and volunteering what's going on inside to stay connected. Your privacy is important to me.

LoSoP Pg 34

WEEK 11:

EMOTIONAL RESPONSIBILITY

Owning our emotions fosters healthy relationships.

In LoSoP, emotional responsibility means owning our emotions and the role we play in our relationships. Instead of blaming others or external circumstances, we take responsibility for how we react and contribute to the connection. This approach encourages personal growth and helps create a culture where individuals are empowered to manage their emotions, leading to healthier, more resilient relationships.

Picture This:

Imagine you're holding a remote control. If someone else has the remote, they can control the volume, change the channel, or turn the TV off. But when you hold the remote, you have control over what's happening. Emotional responsibility is like taking back the remote—owning your actions and reactions, and choosing how to respond in any situation.

Let's Make It Real:

As the presenter, share a time when you took emotional responsibility in a challenging situation. How did it impact the relationship, and what did you learn about your role in maintaining connection?

Discussion Questions:

1. How does taking responsibility for your emotions influence your relationships with students or colleagues?
2. Can you think of a time when avoiding emotional responsibility led to a breakdown in connection? How could it have been handled differently?
3. What steps can you take to practice emotional responsibility in your daily interactions?

Action Goal:

Take responsibility for one emotion or reaction in a challenging situation this week and communicate it to the person involved.

We must deal with our own instinct to react to fear with self-protective behaviors before we can guide our students toward their own emotional awareness and internal sense of responsibility.

LoSoP Pg 31

WEEK 12:

DISCIPLINE OVER PUNISHMENT

Choosing discipline teaches responsibility over fear-based punishment.

In LoSoP, we move away from using punishment as a tool for behaviour management. Instead, we focus on discipline that guides students through their mistakes and teaches them responsibility. Punishment creates fear and disconnection, while discipline, rooted in empathy and understanding, fosters growth and strengthens relationships. By embracing discipline over punishment, we create environments where students feel safe to make mistakes and learn from them.

Picture This:

Imagine a young plant trying to grow. If you constantly strike the plant every time it bends in the wrong direction, it will become damaged and stunted. However, if you gently guide the plant with supports and care, it can grow strong and healthy. The same is true with students—

42

punishment damages their growth, while discipline and support help them thrive.

Let's Make It Real:

In partners, reflect on a time when you used discipline instead of punishment to guide a student or colleague through a challenging situation. How did this approach impact the outcome and the relationship?

Discussion Questions:

1. How does using discipline over punishment impact your relationships with students or colleagues?
2. Can you identify a time when punishment caused disconnection? How could a disciplined approach have helped?
3. What practical steps can you take to create a culture that encourages learning and growth rather than fear and punishment?

Action Goal:

Choose one moment this week to practice discipline instead of punishment by using curiosity to guide a student or colleague.

Our goal isn't simply to teach students information, but to coach them toward being powerful people with a stable and secure sense of self and the habits of approach to manage their emotions and meet their needs. We do this first by role-modeling what it looks like to be secure and powerful ourselves, and then by offering a loving presence with the goal of establishing secure attachment, trust, and empowering discipline in our connection with them.

LoSoP Pg 108

WEEK 13:

EMPATHY IN EDUCATION

Use empathy to support students and colleagues.

Empathy is the ability to understand and share the feelings of another. In LoSoP, empathy is a critical tool for fostering connection and supporting students and colleagues. By putting ourselves in others' shoes, we can better understand their challenges and respond with care and compassion. Empathy helps to create an environment where people feel seen, heard, and supported.

Picture This:

Imagine getting a thorn stuck in your skin. At first, it's a small irritation, something you could remove easily. But if you ignore it, the area becomes infected and swollen, eventually requiring a much more complex procedure to heal. In relationships, unresolved problems can fester in the same way. By ignoring or dismissing someone's emotional pain, it can grow into something more serious. Empathy is like removing the thorn early—acknowledging the issue and addressing it before it becomes a deeper wound that's harder to heal.

Let's Make It Real:

In small groups, reflect on a time when you used empathy to support a student or colleague. How did addressing their needs early help prevent a larger issue? How did empathy change the dynamic of your relationship?

Discussion Questions:

1. How does empathy change the way you interact with students or colleagues?
2. Can you think of a time when a lack of empathy led to disconnection? How could empathy have improved the situation?
3. What are practical ways you can incorporate more empathy into your daily interactions?

Action Goal:

Take time to practice active listening with one student or colleague, focusing on truly understanding their perspective without judgment.

The whole process of creating safety and building a good, strong connection through love and empathy is called "right-to-right brain attunement." This neural connection enables you and your students to feel safe to express emotions, allowing each of you to manage your half of the connection whilst the other person can explore their options.

LoSoP Pg 69

WEEK 14:

AUTHENTICITY IN LEADERSHIP

Lead with honesty and transparency to build trust.

In LoSoP, authenticity is about leading with transparency, honesty, and a genuine desire to connect. Authentic leadership fosters trust and respect, as it encourages people to show up as their true selves. When leaders are authentic, they inspire others to be real and vulnerable, creating an environment where people feel safe to express themselves and build meaningful connections.

Picture This:

Imagine a lighthouse guiding ships through a storm. The light is steady, consistent, and unwavering, offering a clear path to safety. Authentic leadership is like that lighthouse—consistent and true to its values, providing guidance and stability in times of uncertainty.

Let's Make It Real:

In partners, share a time when you showed authenticity in your leadership, either with students or colleagues. How did being real and transparent impact the relationship or situation?

Discussion Questions:

1. How does being authentic in your leadership influence the way others respond to you?
2. Can you think of a time when a lack of authenticity affected your connection with others? How could authenticity have improved the situation?
3. What steps can you take to practice authenticity in your daily leadership?

Action Goal:

Be authentic by sharing a personal story of vulnerability or growth with your team to foster openness and trust.

Central to building trust is, once again, the development of connection.

LoSoP Pg 155

WEEK 15:

INTENTIONAL COMMUNICATION

Be purposeful in communication to foster connection.

Communication is the foundation of all relationships, and in LoSoP, we emphasise the importance of being intentional with our words and actions. Intentional communication means speaking and listening with purpose, ensuring that our interactions are clear, respectful, and aimed at building connection. It involves thinking carefully about how our communication impacts others and making sure it aligns with our values of respect and care.

Picture This:

Imagine you have the choice to either be a turkey or an eagle. The turkey stays close to the ground, making noise but not rising above its surroundings. The eagle, on the other hand, soars high, seeing the bigger picture and moving with purpose. In communication, we have the same choice: we can be reactive and scattered like the turkey, or we can be intentional and purposeful like the eagle. The way we choose to communicate can either elevate the relationship or keep it grounded in misunderstanding and noise.

Let's Make It Real:

Reflect quietly on a recent conversation where your communication either helped you rise above a challenge or kept you grounded in conflict. What could you have done differently to ensure the communication was intentional and purposeful?

Discussion Questions:

1. How does intentional communication affect your relationships with students or colleagues?
2. Can you identify a time when unintentional communication caused disconnection? How could the situation have been handled more effectively?
3. What practical steps can you take to improve your communication and ensure it supports connection?

Action Goal:

Set a goal to pause and think before you respond in a conversation, ensuring that your communication is purposeful and clear.

As long as they are consistently guided towards the goal of respectful communication--largely by us modeling respectful communication-- they will get there.

LoSoP Pg 57

WEEK 16:

FREEDOM THROUGH CHOICES

Giving freedom to make choices empowers responsibility.

In LoSoP, we believe that freedom is a vital part of connection. Giving students and colleagues the freedom to make choices allows them to take ownership of their actions and develop responsibility. Freedom fosters trust, as it communicates respect for the other person's ability to make decisions. When we provide choices, we encourage growth and empower others to take charge of their own learning and behaviour.

Picture This:

Imagine a bird in a cage. While the cage provides safety, it also limits the bird's ability to fly and explore. When the bird is set free, it can soar, discovering new heights. Freedom in relationships works the same way—by allowing others the freedom to choose, we enable them to grow and reach their full potential.

Let's Make It Real:

As the presenter, share a time when you gave a student or colleague the freedom to make choices. How did this approach impact their behaviour, engagement, or connection with you?

Discussion Questions:

1. How does giving freedom through choices impact your relationships with students or colleagues?
2. Can you think of a time when limiting choices caused disconnection? How could providing more freedom have changed the outcome?
3. What are some ways you can incorporate more freedom and choice into your classroom or workplace to foster responsibility and connection?

Action Goal:

Give students or colleagues the freedom to choose their approach to one task this week, allowing them to take ownership of the outcome.

Ultimately, choosing to empower our students with the freedom and responsibility to make their own choices sends them the message of love. As Danny Silk often says, "You cannot have love if you do not have freedom and you do not have freedom if you do not have a choice." Put simply, love requires freedom and freedom requires a choice; therefore, love is a choice.

LoSoP Pg 20

WEEK 17:

THE TRUST CYCLE IN ACTION

Build trust through attuned responses to expressed needs.

In LoSoP, we recognise that trust is built through a fundamental cycle of needs being expressed and met. According to Erik Erikson's theory of psychosocial development, the first task of every child is learning to trust their environment. Danny Silk explains that this task centers around the "trust cycle" a child experiences with their primary caregiver.

The trust cycle begins with a need being identified and expressed. This is followed by the caregiver's response to meet that need, resulting in satisfaction and comfort. When we correctly identify and respond to a student's need, it creates reassurance and fosters trust, making the student more likely to seek us out in the future. Conversely, when needs are unmet or responded to incorrectly, mistrust begins to form, and the relationship becomes insecure.

The trust cycle concept is important in classrooms and leadership relationships because it highlights how attuned responses can build or break trust over time. Transparency and open communication are essential in fostering trust, creating safe spaces where students or colleagues feel understood and valued.

Picture This:

Imagine a young child crying for help. The caregiver responds quickly and accurately, providing comfort. Over time, the child learns that expressing needs leads to them being met, reinforcing trust. In relationships with students or colleagues, being attuned to needs and responding with clarity and care creates the same sense of trust and security.

Let's Make It Real:

In trios, share a time when attuning to a student or colleague's needs helped build trust. Reflect on a moment when responding accurately to someone's needs strengthened the relationship, or alternatively, when a missed cue led to disconnection.

Discussion Questions:

1. How does understanding the trust cycle help you build stronger relationships with students or colleagues?
2. Can you think of a time when a missed opportunity to respond to a need impacted trust? How could this situation have been handled differently?

3. What practical steps can you take to become more attuned to the needs of your students or colleagues to build trust?

Action Goal:

Identify a moment when a student or colleague expresses a need (whether directly or indirectly) and respond with care and transparency, focusing on building or restoring trust.

Danny Silk notes that the behaviors of trust and connection that lead to secure attachment equally endorse freedom and choices within a relationship. He also adds that it is within the safety of a secure attachment that a parent or significant adult can provide a child the best and most effective guidance for making good choices.

LoSoP Pg 93

WEEK 18:

VALUE OF RESPONSIBILITY

Take ownership in relationships and interactions.

In LoSoP, we emphasise the importance of responsibility in relationships. Taking responsibility means owning our part in any interaction, without blaming others or making excuses. By accepting responsibility, we model accountability for students and colleagues, showing them how to build strong, respectful connections. Responsibility also strengthens trust, as it demonstrates integrity and a commitment to maintaining a healthy relationship.

Picture This:

Imagine a boat being rowed by two people. If one person stops rowing, the boat drifts off course. But when both people take responsibility to row, the boat moves smoothly toward its destination. Responsibility in relationships works in the same way—when everyone does their part, the relationship moves forward with purpose and connection.

Let's Make It Real:

In small groups, reflect on a time when you took responsibility for your part in a situation with a student or colleague. How did this change the outcome, and how did it impact the relationship?

Discussion Questions:

1. How does taking responsibility affect your relationships with students or colleagues?
2. Can you think of a time when avoiding responsibility caused tension or disconnection? How could responsibility have changed the situation?
3. What are some practical ways you can demonstrate responsibility in your daily interactions to build stronger connections?

Action Goal:

Model responsibility by acknowledging a mistake or misstep you made this week, demonstrating accountability to others.

This is why we must teach our students how to take responsibility for their own lives and outcomes amidst difficult seasons that will inevitably come. We do this by creating safe places for risks to be taken, messes to be made, learning to occur, problems to be solved, and relationships to be restored through using tools of approach. This gives our students the opportunity to learn that taking responsibility for their own lives is a positive experience that increases happiness and pleasure and can be replicated the next time a mistake or life event happens. I call this level of maturity joyful responsibility.

LoSoP Pg 108

WEEK 19:

WORK HARD AT LOVE

Choose love and connection even when it's challenging.

In LoSoP, love is not just a feeling but an action—a commitment to doing what is best for others. It requires intentional effort, especially in challenging times. Working hard at love means choosing to stay connected, even when it's difficult, and demonstrating love through how we speak and treat others. By consistently showing love, we build stronger, healthier relationships that can withstand challenges.

Picture This:

Imagine a garden that needs regular care. Without watering, pruning, and nurturing, the plants will wither. But with consistent effort and attention, the garden flourishes. Love in relationships is similar—it requires consistent effort to grow and thrive, especially during difficult times.

Let's Make It Real:

As the presenter, share a time when you worked hard at love in a challenging situation with a student or colleague. How did this intentional effort impact the relationship, and what was the outcome?

Discussion Questions:

1. How does working hard at love affect your relationships with students or colleagues?
2. Can you think of a time when you chose to stay connected despite difficulties? What impact did that choice have?
3. What are some practical ways you can work hard at love in your daily interactions?

Action Goal:

Choose one relationship to invest extra time and care into this week, even if it's challenging, by offering an unexpected act of kindness.

Culture of Love: We will work hard at our love and actively express love in how we speak and treat others. We will never turn our love off toward each other.

LoSoP Pg 120

WEEK 20:

CELEBRATING GROWTH

Acknowledging progress fosters motivation and connection.

In LoSoP, we believe in celebrating growth, no matter how small. Growth signifies progress, effort, and learning, and celebrating it helps reinforce positive behaviours and choices. By acknowledging growth in students and colleagues, we send a message that they are seen, valued, and appreciated for their hard work and development. This practice not only strengthens connection but also encourages a culture of continuous improvement.

Picture This:

Think of tracking a child's height on the doorframe and celebrating birthdays or special anniversaries. Each mark on the wall represents growth, and each celebration is a recognition of that progress. We would be devastated if a child stopped growing at 8 years old; instead, we cheer them on as they continue to reach new milestones. In the same way, celebrating growth in students and colleagues, no matter how small, motivates them to keep progressing. Each step forward is worth acknowledging, just like every new mark on the doorframe is a reason to celebrate.

Let's Make It Real:

Open invite: Anyone who feels comfortable is welcome to share a moment of personal or professional growth they've experienced recently. How did recognising and celebrating that growth affect your connection with others?

Discussion Questions:

1. How does celebrating growth, no matter how small, impact your relationships with students or colleagues?
2. Can you identify a time when celebrating someone's progress led to increased motivation and connection?
3. What are some practical ways you can celebrate growth in your classroom or workplace on a regular basis?

Action Goal:

Identify and celebrate a specific area of growth in a student or colleague this week, even if it's small, and acknowledge their effort.

There is no higher or better motivation for our behavior. Love is the superior driver of all learning, growth, problem-solving, achievement, and productivity.

LoSoP Pg 26

WEEK 21:

STRENGTHENING RELATIONSHIPS THROUGH CO-REGULATION

Predictable actions and emotional support create stable connections.

In LoSoP, relationships are built through predictable, supportive actions. A key aspect is co-regulation, where teachers help students manage emotions by providing stability and presence. This process teaches self-regulation, essential for long-term emotional health.

Often, students are taught to regulate emotions through external distractions, like phones, fidget toys, or snacks—this is object regulation. While these quick fixes provide short-term relief, they don't build the internal skills needed for emotional growth. Over time, reliance on such distractions can lead to unhealthy coping mechanisms. In contrast, co-regulation involves being present with students during stress, using voice, gestures, and tone to help them feel understood and learn how to self-soothe without rescuing them.

Teachers play a crucial role in this process by creating supportive, calm environments that model self-regulation, whether through breathing exercises or simply providing a steady presence during challenging moments.

Picture This:

Imagine teaching someone to ride a bike. At first, you hold the seat, guiding them as they wobble. With every attempt, they gain more balance, until they eventually ride on their own, confident and steady. This process mirrors co-regulation. You are present, offering guidance without taking over, allowing them to build the skills they need for independence. Now, imagine if instead, you gave them training wheels indefinitely. While it would keep them upright, they'd never learn the balance required to ride independently.

Let's Make It Real:

In partners, discuss the balance of object regulation versus co-regulation in your environment. How often are distractions or quick fixes used to soothe, and how could more intentional co-regulation strategies be implemented to create stronger, healthier connections?

Discussion Questions:

1. How do you recognise moments where object regulation is being used in your classroom or among colleagues?
2. Can you recall a time when co-regulation helped build a stronger connection with a student or colleague? How did this impact their emotional growth and your relationship?

3. What practical steps can you take to promote co-regulation in your daily interactions?

Action Goal:

This week, practice co-regulation by being present and attuned during a challenging moment with a student or colleague rather than offering quick-fix distractions.

Self-regulation then is what we want all of our graduates to master. Self-regulation is just that--the ability to regulate your own feelings, thoughts, or actions associated with distress and return them to homeostasis.

LoSoP Pg 103

WEEK 22:

NURTURING A CULTURE OF CARE

Create an environment where everyone feels valued and supported.

In LoSoP, nurturing a culture of care means creating an environment where students and colleagues feel safe, valued, and supported. This involves showing empathy, listening attentively, and offering help when needed. A culture of care encourages individuals to be their best selves, as they know they are supported by the people around them. It strengthens relationships and fosters a sense of belonging and community.

Picture This:

Think of the redwood forest, where the tallest trees in the world stand strong not because of their individual roots, but because their roots intertwine with one another. The trees hold each other up, creating a network of support that keeps the entire forest thriving. In the same way, when we create a culture of care, we are like those interconnected roots, providing support and strength for everyone in our community. When one person leans on another, the entire group grows stronger together.

Let's Make It Real:

As the presenter, share a time when you intentionally nurtured a culture of care in your classroom or workplace. How did this approach impact the people around you, and what changes did you notice in the environment?

Discussion Questions:

1. How does creating a culture of care impact your relationships with students or colleagues?
2. Can you think of a time when a lack of care affected the environment or relationships? How could this have been addressed?
3. What practical steps can you take to foster a culture of care in your daily interactions?

Action Goal:

Perform one act of care this week, such as offering help or support to someone in need, and encourage others to do the same.

Most of all, I want to see you developing your internal character and a secure identity in which you know that you are worthy to be loved, chosen, and cherished.

LoSoP Pg 161

WEEK 23:

BEHAVIOUR EDUCATION: RESPECT AND RESPONSIBILITY

How we approach behaviour shapes relationships and fosters responsibility.

In LoSoP, the way we explain and enforce school behaviour policies speaks volumes about our intentions—whether we aim to control and punish or to connect and empower. Behaviour education is deeply connected to respect and responsibility, and the way we handle disrespectful or inappropriate behaviour can either foster connection or breed rebellion.

As Danny Silk often quotes from Josh McDowell, 'Rules without relationship lead to rebellion'. He expands on this with, 'Rules within relationship equal respect and responsibility'. This perfectly captures the tension in many classrooms and school environments. The balance between enforcing rules and fostering relationships is key to promoting respect and responsibility in students.

Picture This:

Imagine a graph with two axes—one representing Rules & Responsibility, and the other representing Relationship & Connection. Where these two intersect is where respect and responsibility thrive. If we only focus on rules without building relationships, students may comply out of fear, but true responsibility doesn't develop. However, when we combine clear boundaries with meaningful connections, students feel empowered to take responsibility for their actions.

Let's Make It Real:

In small groups, discuss a time when the way you enforced rules either built connection or led to disconnection with a student. Reflect on how balancing responsibility with relationship could have changed the outcome.

Discussion Questions:

1. How does the way we communicate and enforce behaviour policies impact respect and responsibility in students?
2. Can you think of a time when rules were enforced without relationship, and how it affected behaviour? What could have been done differently to foster connection?
3. What practical steps can you take to promote both respect and responsibility through connection in your classroom or workplace?

Action Goal:

This week, identify a behavioural issue and, instead of focusing solely on punishment, approach it with the goal of connecting and empowering the student to take responsibility.

Both teachers and students have a clear blueprint to orient themselves each day in connection with one another. In this way, students and teachers participate in a predictable sequence of behavior education that removes "offense" and instead puts the situation in front of each person to reflect on and adjust.

LoSoP Pg 151

WEEK 24:

CONNECTION BEYOND COMFORT ZONES

Build connections by stepping outside familiar circles.

In LoSoP, we emphasise the importance of building connections beyond the people we naturally gravitate toward. Strong relationships often develop when we step outside our comfort zones and reach out to those we may not know well. By intentionally connecting with others, we can build a more inclusive and connected community where everyone feels valued and seen.

Picture This:

Imagine an above-ground whirlpool—strong and energetic, pulling people toward the centre. When a culture of connection is strong, it naturally draws in those around it, inviting people to be part of the flow. But if we only connect with those already close to us and ignore others on the outside, the whirlpool weakens and people stop being drawn in. To keep the whirlpool strong, we must step outside our comfort zones and make sure everyone feels included in the flow of connection.

Let's Make It Real:

Pair up with someone you don't know very well and share a story about a time when stepping outside your comfort zone helped you build a new connection. How did that experience impact your relationships, and what did you learn about the importance of including others in the process of connection?

Discussion Questions:

1. How does stepping outside your comfort zone affect your ability to build meaningful connections?
2. Can you think of a time when you avoided connecting with someone new? How might reaching out have changed the situation?
3. What are some practical steps you can take to build connections with those outside your usual circle?

Action Goal:

Make an effort to connect with someone outside your usual circle this week by initiating a conversation or collaboration.

If students become more likely to avoid new experiences because they perceive true pleasure and comfort comes from "staying the same," then the establishment of new learning can be stunted.

LoSoP Pg 99

WEEK 25:

CONNECTION THROUGH ACTIVE LISTENING

Active listening is key to deeper connections.

Active listening is a crucial part of building strong relationships in LoSoP. It involves fully focusing on the speaker, understanding their message, and responding thoughtfully. When we practice active listening, we show respect and care for the person we're engaging with, which strengthens trust and connection. It's not just about hearing words but about truly understanding the emotions and needs behind them.

Picture This:

Imagine a musician tuning their instrument before a concert. They listen intently, adjusting each string until the sound is perfect. In conversations, active listening is like that fine-tuning—it ensures that we are aligned with the person speaking, creating harmony in the relationship.

Let's Make It Real:

As the presenter, share a story about a time when active listening helped you connect with a student or colleague. How did fully listening to them change the dynamic of the relationship, and what impact did it have on the outcome of the situation?

Discussion Questions:

1. How does active listening strengthen your relationships with students or colleagues?
2. Can you think of a time when a lack of listening led to disconnection? How could active listening have changed the situation?
3. What steps can you take to become a better active listener in your daily interactions?

Action Goal:

Practice active listening with one person this week by giving them your full attention and withholding judgment during the conversation.

"Bernii, why do the students you work with listen to you? I have been watching you (said Ruth). They don't listen to their teachers. Some of them don't even listen to their parents. But when you speak with them, they tell you the truth and they take responsibility. What are you doing?"

I almost fell over backwards. Instead, I whispered back, "Would you like to borrow the training I did on DVD?"

"Yes, please."

The next time I saw Ruth, I silently handed her a copy of the Loving our Kids on Purpose DVDs.

LoSoP Pg 244

WEEK 26:

PREDICTABILITY IN CONNECTION

Being reliable and predictable builds trust.

In LoSoP, predictability is key to maintaining strong and healthy relationships. Predictability means showing up regularly with care, trust, and respect, even when it's challenging. When we are predictable in our interactions with students and colleagues, we create a stable environment where connection can grow. Unpredictable behaviour can lead to confusion and disconnection, but predictability builds trust over time.

Picture This:

Think of the difference between instant coffee and a barista-made coffee. Instant coffee is quick and easy, but it lacks the richness and quality of a carefully crafted coffee made by a barista, who takes time to prepare each cup with care. Both are predictable—you know what to expect. Every day, you have a choice: will you offer barista-made predictability, which takes time, effort, and attention but leads to deeper, richer connections? Instant solutions may be convenient, but they don't create the same level of trust and reliability.

Let's Make It Real:

In partners, reflect on a time when being predictable helped you build a stronger connection with a student or colleague. How did being reliable and steady impact your relationship, and what did you learn from the experience?

Discussion Questions:

1. How does predictability impact your relationships with students or colleagues?
2. Can you think of a time when unpredictability led to disconnection? How could predictability have helped?
3. What practical steps can you take to be more predictable in your daily interactions?

Action Goal:

Commit to one predictable action, such as regular check-ins with students or colleagues, to strengthen relationships over time.

This allows students of all ages to be able to predict my movements and help them understand my intention to make them feel safe and connect with them. In short, I am building trust by providing consistent cues for how I will behave around them and removing unpredictability that comes from a reactive temperament, sarcasm, misplaced teasing, and public shaming.

LoSoP Pg 68

WEEK 27:

POWERFUL TEACHERS SAY LESS: ONE-LINERS

Use simple phrases to avoid power struggles and encourage responsibility.

In LoSoP, staying powerful in the classroom often means saying less and avoiding unnecessary power struggles. When students argue or push boundaries, it's easy to get drawn into an argument, but powerful teachers know how to stay composed and let students engage with themselves. The use of one-liners from Love and Logic (2005) by Jim Faye and Foster Cline is a simple, effective strategy to maintain calm, foster connection, and encourage responsibility.

These memorable one-liners include:

"I know."   "Probably so."   "That may be."   "I don't know."
"Nice try."

By using these phrases, teachers can avoid escalating arguments, maintain a positive atmosphere, and guide students without getting into a battle of wills. These one-liners allow teachers to acknowledge a student's frustration while holding them accountable without becoming emotionally involved in the debate. They are especially useful when students are pushing boundaries or not meeting expectations, as they offer a way to respond without sending negative or disempowering messages.

Picture This:

Imagine a student coming up with reasons why they shouldn't have to follow a classroom rule. The teacher simply responds with, "That may be" or "Nice try," defusing the argument without engaging in a back-and-forth. The student soon realises they aren't going to win the debate, and the teacher remains calm and in control, all while reinforcing expectations.

Let's Make It Real:

In small groups, reflect on a time when you could have used one-liners to avoid an argument or defuse a situation with a student. Share how you could apply these phrases to maintain a sense of connection and responsibility in future situations.

Discussion Questions:

1. How can using one-liners help you maintain your composure and stay out of power struggles with students?
2. Can you think of a time when engaging in an argument with a student could have been avoided by saying less?
3. What are some practical steps you can take to start using one-liners in your classroom or workplace?

Action Goal:

Practice using one-liners with your students this week. Focus on remaining calm and composed, allowing the student to engage with their own choices rather than engaging in a debate.

You need to have a plan. You need to know what your response is going to be when their behavior catches you off guard.

LoSoP Pg 167

WEEK 28:

RECOGNISING FALSE CONNECTIONS

True connection is built on trust, not manipulation or control.

In LoSoP, it's important to understand the difference between true connections and false connections. A false connection may appear strong on the surface, but it lacks the depth and honesty that comes from mutual trust and understanding. False connections often arise when people use manipulation, fear, or control to maintain relationships, rather than fostering genuine respect and care. Recognising and moving away from false connections allows us to create more authentic, meaningful relationships.

Picture This:

Imagine a bridge that looks sturdy from a distance, but upon closer inspection, it's held together by weak materials. The bridge might seem strong, but it won't hold up under pressure. In relationships, false connections are like that weak bridge—they may look fine on the surface, but they lack the foundation needed to last.

Let's Make It Real:

In small groups, reflect on a time when you recognised a false connection in your personal or professional life. How did it affect the relationship, and what steps did you take to move toward a more genuine connection?

Discussion Questions:

1. How can you recognise the signs of a false connection in your relationships with students or colleagues?
2. Can you think of a time when a false connection created tension or disconnection? How could that have been prevented?
3. What practical steps can you take to foster more genuine, authentic connections in your daily interactions?

Action Goal:

Reflect on a relationship where connection feels forced or shallow, and take one step toward making it more authentic.

For teachers laboring under the false belief of control, it is painful when they start to discover they do not control the next thing that comes out of a student's mouth, the next thing they do with their hands, the next thing they learn. Nor do I.

LoSoP Pg 31

WEEK 29:

TRUSTING THE PROCESS OF CONNECTION

Building connection takes time, patience, and commitment.

In LoSoP, building and maintaining connection is seen as a process that requires patience, understanding, and commitment. Trusting the process means acknowledging that relationships take time to develop and that setbacks are a natural part of the journey. When we trust the process, we remain committed to the goal of connection, even when challenges arise. This trust helps us navigate difficult moments and reinforces the bonds we're building.

Picture This:

Think of a time when you've been following GPS directions, only to lose signal and miss your turn. You may feel frustrated and lost, but the GPS will always recalculate and guide you back on track. In relationships, connection works the same way—sometimes we lose our way, but by trusting the process and recalculating our steps, we can find our way back to a stronger, more aligned relationship.

Let's Make It Real:

Reflect with your direct team on a time when trusting the process of connection helped strengthen relationships in your classroom or workplace. How did patience and persistence contribute to a deeper, more lasting connection?

Discussion Questions:

1. How does trusting the process of connection impact your relationships with students or colleagues?
2. Can you think of a time when impatience or frustration hindered the process of building connection? How could trusting the process have changed the outcome?
3. What steps can you take to remind yourself and your team to trust the process of building and maintaining connections?

Action Goal:

Be patient with a relationship that is developing slowly, and trust the process by offering consistent support without rushing the outcome.

We are after teaching our students the value and power of relationship and love, not about compliance or obedience.

LoSoP Pg 150

WEEK 30:

THE POWER OF CURIOSITY
OVER CONTROL

Curiosity opens the door to empathy and connection.

In LoSoP, curiosity is a powerful tool for building connections, especially when things are challenging. Instead of trying to control situations or people, asking questions and showing genuine interest in understanding what's going on can lead to better outcomes. Curiosity opens the door to empathy and connection, while control creates tension and disconnection. By being curious, we allow space for growth, learning, and mutual respect.

Picture This:

Imagine you're driving down a road and suddenly hit a detour. You can either force your way through, trying to find shortcuts and getting frustrated, or you can take the time to explore the new route with curiosity, discovering new things along the way. Curiosity in relationships is like taking that detour with an open mind, leading to new insights and deeper connections.

Let's Make It Real:

As the presenter, share a time when you used curiosity instead of control in a challenging situation. How did this approach change the outcome, and what impact did it have on the relationship with the student or colleague?

Discussion Questions:

1. How does choosing curiosity over control affect your relationships with students or colleagues?
2. Can you think of a time when control caused disconnection? How could curiosity have changed the situation?
3. What steps can you take to practice curiosity more intentionally in your daily interactions?

Action Goal:

Approach a challenging situation this week with curiosity instead of control, and ask open-ended questions to explore possible solutions.

As I observe students, I am constantly asking questions about their safety stool. What needs are they expressing through their behavior? Is our attachment secure, our brains attuned, and our hearts connected? What are they trying to control in their environment? Are they trying to orientate themselves to the new environment of our school? Are they under the illusion that they can control me or their teachers? Is there an issue around pleasure and pain? Are they avoiding being embarrassed by having to read in front of their friends so they don't want to put their hand up? Are they making jokes so that their friends will laugh at them and they don't feel incompetent?

LoSoP Pg 108

WEEK 31:

EMPOWERING THROUGH CHOICES

Offering choices fosters independence and responsibility.

In LoSoP, empowering students and colleagues means giving them the freedom to make choices and take responsibility for their actions. Empowerment is about trust—trusting that others can make decisions and learn from their experiences. When we offer choices, we not only foster independence but also build stronger, more respectful relationships. This approach creates a culture where people feel valued and confident in their ability to contribute.

Picture This:

Imagine playing a video game where you're given multiple choices that affect the outcome of the story. The more choices you're allowed to make, the more invested you become in the game's outcome. Empowering others through choices works the same way—when people have the freedom to choose, they become more engaged and invested in their growth and relationships.

Let's Make It Real:

Share with the person next to you a time when you empowered someone by giving them a choice. How did this impact their behaviour or engagement, and what effect did it have on your relationship?

Discussion Questions:

1. How does giving choices empower students or colleagues and strengthen relationships?
2. Can you think of a time when taking away choices led to disconnection? How could offering choices have changed the outcome?
3. What are some practical ways you can empower others through choices in your daily interactions?

Action Goal:

Empower someone this week by giving them a meaningful choice in a task or decision, allowing them to take ownership.

Applied neuroscience confirmed what I was observing in classrooms and student relationships––specifically, that creating safe environments void of fear and punishment, environments where students feel connected and empowered as they take responsibility for their own learning, increases the brain's ability to learn, take risks, and develop resilience.

LoSoP Pg 18

WEEK 32:

BUILDING RESILIENCE THROUGH CONNECTION

Connection supports resilience in overcoming challenges.

In LoSoP, connection is key to building resilience. Resilience is the ability to recover from difficulties and setbacks, and strong relationships play a vital role in this process. When students or colleagues know they have a supportive and caring network, they are more likely to bounce back from challenges. Building resilience through connection creates an environment where people feel safe to grow, learn, and persevere, even in the face of adversity.

Picture This:

Imagine a trampoline. The tighter and more secure the springs are, the higher you can bounce back after falling. In relationships, connection is like those springs—it gives people the strength to recover and rise after setbacks. The stronger the connection, the more resilient people become.

Let's Make It Real:

In small groups, reflect on a time when connection helped you or someone else build resilience after a difficult situation. How did the support of others help you recover, and what did you learn about the importance of connection in challenging times?

Discussion Questions:

1. How does building connection help foster resilience in students or colleagues?
2. Can you think of a time when a lack of connection made it harder to bounce back from a challenge? How could connection have helped?
3. What steps can you take to strengthen connections and build resilience in your classroom or workplace?

Action Goal:

Provide encouragement and support to someone going through a tough time this week, helping them to build resilience through your connection.

A poor choice is just that--a poor choice. When students learn how to clean up their poor choices to ensure that nobody gets hurt by it, they are developing complex life skills that will set them up for resilience and success as an adult. They learn that they are not a mistake, but they make mistakes. They learn that they can keep building something beautiful, despite their mistakes.

LoSoP Pg 156

WEEK 33:

LOVE IS A CHOICE, NOT A FEELING

Love is an intentional act, not just an emotion.

In LoSoP, we teach that love is not just a feeling but a conscious choice. Choosing love means consistently acting in ways that are respectful, kind, and supportive, even when it's difficult. This perspective shifts love from being something passive to something we actively decide to do. By choosing love, we create a culture where relationships are built on respect and intentional care, rather than fleeting emotions.

Picture This:

Imagine you're an artist painting a mural. Each stroke is a deliberate choice, contributing to the final masterpiece. Love is like those brush-strokes—each action you take contributes to the larger picture of connection and care, shaping the relationships you build.

Let's Make It Real:

Reflect quietly on a time when you made the choice to show love in a difficult situation. How did that choice impact the relationship, and what did you learn about the power of love as a decision rather than a feeling?

Discussion Questions:

1. How does viewing love as a choice change your approach to relationships with students or colleagues?
2. Can you think of a time when choosing not to love affected your relationship with someone? How could the situation have been different?
3. What are some practical ways you can choose love in your daily interactions, even when it's challenging?

Action Goal:

Make a conscious choice to act with love and kindness toward someone this week, even in a challenging situation.

Connection doesn't just happen—it is something we cultivate through our choices. Love is not just a feeling. It is the powerful choice to treat others in a certain way, whether or not they are loving us in return.

LoSoP Pg 27

WEEK 34:

GENUINE TRANSFORMATION—CLEANING UP MESSES

Guide students beyond confession toward true transformation of mind and behaviour.

In LoSoP, we aim for a greater goal than confession and punishment. While admitting a mistake is part of the process, true transformation comes when students take joyful responsibility for their choices and clean up their messes. This transformation happens at a cognitive and neural level, requiring a change in thinking and behaviour.

Genuine transformation is not about quick fixes or superficial confessions. Real change requires guiding students through a process of reflection, responsibility, and behavioural adjustment. This is where boundaries come into play. Unlike walls that communicate rejection, boundaries protect relationships and invite students to take responsibility for their actions, restoring connection in the process.

Picture This:

Danny Silk uses the story of Simba from The Lion King to illustrate this transformation. Simba, filled with shame and fear of punishment, flees his responsibility as king. Through the support of Nala and Rafiki, Simba remembers his worth and true identity, which shifts his behaviour from avoidance to action, and he restores the pride.

Let's Make It Real:

In small groups, discuss a time when you helped a student move beyond confession toward true transformation. How did the process of reflection and responsibility impact the student's behaviour and your relationship with them?

Discussion Questions:

1. How does guiding students toward genuine transformation differ from simply accepting an apology or confession?
2. Can you think of a time when a student confessed or apologised but didn't change their behaviour? What could have been done differently to guide them toward transformation?
3. What practical steps can you take to apply boundaries that encourage responsibility and transformation in your classroom or workplace?

Action Goal:

Identify a situation this week where a student or colleague needs to clean up a mess. Instead of focusing on confession or punishment, guide them through a process of reflection, responsibility, and genuine transformation.

Restoration and reconciliation require the combination of genuine forgiveness and repentance. Together these produce transformation. It requires the two people to build a new relational connection. We have the privilege to forgive and support our students as they become freed from their past and who they thought they were, empowered to develop a new internal identity, forgive themselves, transform their thinking, and restore their relationships by choosing connection as their goal. Meanwhile, we are inviting them toward this goal every step of the way because connection is our goal too.

LoSoP Pg 160

WEEK 35:

TRUSTING OTHERS WITH RESPONSIBILITY

Sharing responsibility builds trust and accountability.

In LoSoP, trusting others with responsibility is a powerful way to build connection and foster growth. When we trust students or colleagues with important tasks or decisions, we communicate that we believe in their abilities. This trust empowers them to take ownership of their actions and fosters a sense of pride and accountability. It also strengthens the relationship by showing that we respect their potential and are willing to share responsibility.

Picture This:

Imagine a relay race where one runner must pass the baton to the next. For the race to succeed, the first runner must trust the second to carry the baton forward. In relationships, passing responsibility is like handing off that baton—it shows faith in the other person's ability to carry it forward, building trust and connection.

Let's Make It Real:

As the presenter, share a story about a time when you trusted some-one with responsibility. How did that choice affect your relationship with the person, and what impact did it have on their growth and development?

Discussion Questions:

1. How does trusting others with responsibility impact your rela-tionships with students or colleagues?
2. Can you think of a time when withholding responsibility led to disconnection or frustration? How could sharing responsibili-ty have changed the outcome?
3. What are some practical ways you can begin to trust others with more responsibility in your classroom or workplace?

Action Goal:

Trust someone with a task or responsibility this week that stretches their capabilities, offering them your support along the way.

Little by little, we are building it up, teaching our students how to stay connected during conflict, how to step out of the role of powerless victim and how to take responsibility for their actions. We are preparing them to be incredible employees and business managers, loving spouses, and powerful parents. More than that, as your students learn how to turn their hearts to their teachers and parents, you will have the pleasure of witnessing their parents turning their hearts back toward their children. Our families will create a new normal that will impact generations to come.

LoSoP Pg 123

WEEK 36:

FOSTERING INDEPENDENCE THROUGH CONNECTION

Empower students while maintaining responsibility for your side of the connection.

In LoSoP, fostering independence is key to building strong, empowered connections. A powerful teacher knows how to recognise and name their emotions, understands their own needs, and communicates them clearly. They send the message, "I will manage me while you manage you," and they take responsibility only for their side of the connection. This helps students develop independence, knowing that their teacher trusts them to handle their own choices while offering support.

Independence doesn't mean abandoning students—it means providing the tools and confidence they need to thrive. By recognizing that there is a line where their life stops and another person's life starts, powerful teachers help students develop self-reliance, trust, and responsibility.

Picture This:

Think of teaching someone how to ride a bike. At first, you hold onto the bike to keep it steady, but as they gain confidence, you gradually let go. Letting go isn't about disconnecting; it's about trusting them to use what they've learned to ride on their own. Similarly, a powerful teacher maintains responsibility for themselves while fostering independence in students, ensuring that the relationship stays strong even as students grow more self-reliant.

Let's Make It Real:

In partners, share a time when you fostered independence in a student or colleague while maintaining your side of the connection. How did this approach impact their growth and your relationship with them?

Discussion Questions:

1. How does fostering independence while managing your own side of the connection impact your relationships with students or colleagues?
2. Can you think of a time when a lack of independence hindered someone's growth? How could you have handled it differently while maintaining responsibility for your side of the connection?

3. What practical steps can you take to support independence while clearly managing your emotions and needs in the class-room or workplace?

Action Goal:

Give a student or colleague the space to be independent on a task this week, while ensuring you manage your side of the connection and communicate your needs clearly.

The powerful teacher takes responsibility for their side of the connection and no more. Most importantly, they understand that there is a line where their life stops and another person's life starts.

LoSoP Pg 155

WEEK 37:

ENCOURAGING RISK-TAKING IN
A SAFE ENVIRONMENT

Creating a safe space encourages growth and learning through risk-taking.

In LoSoP, taking risks is an important part of growth and learning. However, for students or colleagues to feel comfortable taking risks, they need to know they are in a safe, supportive environment. Encouraging risk-taking means providing reassurance that mistakes are part of the process and that they will not face judgment or punishment for trying something new. This balance between support and challenge fosters innovation, confidence, and deeper connections.

Picture This:

Imagine a child swimming in the deep end of a pool. Instead of panicking, she pushes off the bottom of the pool to propel herself upward, taking a breath before sinking again and repeating the process. Each time she pushes off, she gets her bearings, gradually moving toward the safety of the pool's edge. This demonstrates how, when faced with challenges, students can push off their lowest points to gain perspective and navigate toward safety, knowing they are supported in the process.

Let's Make It Real:

Share with someone you don't know very well about a time when you encouraged a student or colleague to take a risk in a safe environment. How did creating that sense of safety impact their willingness to take the risk, and what was the outcome?

Discussion Questions:

1. How does creating a safe environment for risk-taking impact your relationships with students or colleagues?
2. Can you think of a time when fear of failure or judgment prevented someone from taking a risk? How could you have made the environment safer for them?
3. What steps can you take to encourage risk-taking while providing support and safety in your daily interactions?

Action Goal:

Encourage someone to take a small, calculated risk this week, reassuring them that it's okay to fail and that you're there to support them.

Imagine releasing young people encultured in love out into our communities around the world--young people who know how to be powerful people, who are not afraid, who can handle large amounts of freedom, who understand the importance of risk and healthy conflict, who honor differences, and who will teach all of this to the next generation.

LoSoP Pg 256

WEEK 38:

FIXING A DISCONNECT––CLEANING UP MESSES

Recognise disconnection and take responsibility to restore relationships.

In LoSoP, we acknowledge that disconnection is an inevitable part of relationships, whether in the classroom or among colleagues. The important question becomes: What do we do when we experience disconnection? Often, a disconnect doesn't require a catastrophised reaction or withdrawal into self-preservation. Instead, it's an opportunity to recognise the issue, take responsibility, and clean up the mess.

The Lego Castle Metaphor:

Imagine that each day is like building a Lego castle. Every choice we make adds a piece to the structure, building something beautiful. Sometimes, we pick a Lego piece that just doesn't fit. We need to decide whether to keep forcing that piece or set it aside. If we leave that piece on the floor without cleaning up our mess, someone might step on it—everyone knows how much stepping on a Lego hurts! One bad moment, like a poor choice in class, shouldn't define the entire day. Just because one piece doesn't fit doesn't mean we throw away the whole castle.

Picture This:

Imagine a student who makes a poor choice and spends the rest of the day focused on that one mistake. Instead of recognising the other good choices they've made, the focus shifts to the one error, potentially ruining the whole day. By teaching them to clean up the mess from that mistake—apologising, taking responsibility, and moving forward—we help them see that they are capable of continuing to build something meaningful.

Let's Make It Real:

In trios, share a time when a disconnect occurred with a student, colleague, or even yourself. Discuss how cleaning up the mess restored the connection and what was learned from the experience.

Discussion Questions:

1. How does recognising a disconnect and cleaning up the mess help restore relationships?
2. Can you think of a time when a small mistake overshadowed an otherwise good day? How could focusing on cleaning up that mistake have helped?

3. What practical steps can you take to help students, or yourself, clean up messes and take responsibility in the future?

Action Goal:

Practice cleaning up your own messes this week by acknowledging a disconnect, taking responsibility, and working to restore the relationship, whether with a student, colleague, or even yourself.

*So we need to get good at recognizing when a disconnect has occurred,
manage our half of the relationship, and clean up any mess so that we
can restore the connection. We need to get good at cleaning up our
own messes and get alongside students to coach them on
how to clean up their own messes.*

LoSoP Pg 157

WEEK 39:

WALKING THROUGH MESSES––BUILDING DEEP CONNECTIONS

Transformation comes from walking through the toughest challenges.

In LoSoP, walking with students or families through their toughest moments can feel daunting, but it also creates an opportunity for deeper connection and transformation. Much like a doctor guiding a woman through pregnancy and delivery, stepping into a place of vulnerability with a student fosters a bond of trust. The students who bring the most excitement with their successes are often those who have walked through the deepest valleys with us. Confrontation, rather than something to fear, becomes a powerful process that leads to genuine transformation.

In schools, big messes can feel overwhelming, and the instinct may be to respond with harsh punishments, such as suspensions or expulsions. But what if there were other options? Before resorting to drastic measures, schools can explore alternatives that help students take responsibility, learn from their mistakes, and grow without severing the connection that's been built.

Picture This:

Think of a cartoon where one character hits another with a small hammer, and the second character responds by pulling out an even bigger hammer to strike back harder. In real life, responding to big messes with big punishments can feel like escalating the conflict, but what if, instead of bigger punishments, we chose a path of support and guidance? Just as a doctor stays with their patient through every step, we can walk with students through their messes, ensuring they learn, grow, and transform through the process.

Let's Make It Real:

Reflect in small groups on a time when you walked with a student or family through a challenging situation. How did this journey strengthen your connection, and what did you learn about the process of supporting them through the mess?

Discussion Questions:

1. How does walking through messes with students or families impact your relationship with them?
2. Can you think of a time when responding with punishment alone might have escalated the situation? How could a more supportive approach have led to a better outcome?

3. What steps can you take to guide students through tough situations in a way that encourages growth and connection rather than fear and punishment?

Action Goal:

Identify a student or family going through a challenging situation and explore ways to support them in cleaning up the mess while fostering deeper connection and trust.

In schools when big messes happen it can be scary. It can be tempting to respond to a big mess with a big punishment.

LoSoP Pg 188

WEEK 40:

CONNECTION AS THE FOUNDATION OF LEADERSHIP

Effective leadership is built on strong relationships, not fear.

In LoSoP, the foundation of effective leadership in the classroom is heart-to-heart connection. Showing vulnerability doesn't mean falling apart or placing too much responsibility on students; it means giving them honest feedback about how their behaviour affects others and communicating what adjustments are needed to protect the connection. This approach empowers students to choose connection over fear, fostering a classroom environment based on mutual respect and care.

The ultimate goal of this type of leadership is creating a space where students instinctively adjust their behaviour because they can see how it impacts the teacher and their peers. A powerful teacher leads with love and communicates through heart-to-heart connections. It's not about giving the "evil eye" but about maintaining a bond so strong that simple eye contact reminds students of the connection they want to protect. This is the true power of relationship-based leadership—students learn to value connection, and compliance becomes a natural result, not the primary objective.

Picture This:

Imagine answering a classroom phone, and all you need to do is make eye contact with your students. Without a word, they instinctively adjust their noise level and take ownership of their behaviour because they can see in your eyes how they are affecting you. This isn't about control or obedience—it's about cultivating a deep understanding that connection is worth protecting.

Let's Make It Real:

Reflect with a partner on a time when you gave students honest feedback about how their behaviour affected the classroom. How did it impact their response, and how did it influence the connection you had with them?

Discussion Questions:

1. How does showing vulnerability help your students take responsibility for their actions and protect the connection in the classroom?
2. Can you think of a time when fear or disconnection affected behaviour in your classroom? How might fostering a heart-to-heart connection have changed the outcome?

3. What practical steps can you take to cultivate this heart-to-heart connection with your students?

Action Goal:

Practice giving honest, vulnerable feedback to your students this week, showing them how their behaviour affects you and others, and encouraging them to choose connection over disconnection.

The beauty of establishing this heart-to-heart connection is that it enables us to lead with love. The Holy Grail of this kind of leadership is getting to the point where your students can simply look into your eyes, know how they are affecting your heart, and adjust their behavior accordingly.

LoSoP Pg 33

ABOUT THE AUTHOR

Bernii Godwin holds a Master's qualification in Social Work and a Graduate Certificate in Neuropsychotherapy, building on her undergraduate degree in Human Services and Criminology and Criminal Justice, with a focus on youth and family justice. She is also a certified Loving on Purpose Trainer and John Maxwell Leadership Team Member.

Over the past two decades, Bernii has worked in various roles across a wide range of schools, specializing in student well-being and behaviour. Principals frequently seek her expertise to consult on complex behaviour and well-being issues, provide one-on-one coaching or supervision to educators and well-being teams, and deliver school-wide professional development. Her greatest passion is helping schools adopt practical tools that replace fear and punishment with purposeful behaviour education, safe connections, and empowered teachers—ultimately increasing student engagement in their academic journey.

To connect with Bernii, please visit
www.godwinconsulting.com.au

COMING SOON

CULTURAL ARCHITECT: CREATING SUSTAINABLE CULTURES FOR LASTING IMPACT

In Cultural Architect: Creating Sustainable Cultures for Lasting Impact, school leaders are offered a revolutionary blueprint to transform their educational environments into vibrant, thriving communities. Drawing from the Sustainable Culture Model, this book provides a practical roadmap to overcome the common challenges of fragmented, inconsistent, or unsustainable school cultures.

Bernii Godwin introduces the transformative power of the LoSoP (Loving Our Students on Purpose) philosophy, which serves as the cornerstone of this model, empowering principals and leadership teams to foster shared values and consistent behaviour that breathe life into school communities.

Whether you're striving for stronger staff engagement, student success, or overall school cohesion, Cultural Architect delivers the tools, strategies, and insights to build cultures that not only inspire today but stand the test of time. This book is essential for those committed to leading with purpose, creating environments where both educators and students can flourish.

What others are saying:

Monica Lemke – Educator & Mom, Texas, USA

'I cannot recommend the LoSoP School Representative Program enough for educators looking to enhance their ability to maintain positive, healthy relationships with their students. The tools and strategies provided have been incredibly valuable in helping me foster a supportive and nurturing environment during my season as a stay-at-home mom. This program is packed with practical tips you can implement immediately, but more than that, it offers a new perspective on how to approach students, coworkers, parents, and even yourself. If teaching no longer feels like a rewarding profession, take this course and rediscover the joy in it. Thank you for creating such a beneficial program for educators!'

Connie Jakab B.R.Ed – Author of Bring Them Closer, Alberta, Canada

'I joined the LoSoP School Reps group to enhance my understanding of the LoSoP framework, and I was blown away by how much the experience exceeded my expectations. It wasn't just a sit-and-learn event; it was interactive, learn-by-doing training. I now have a greater understanding of the powerful teacher, behaviour education, and the empowerment model, and I am confident in leading others through these essential components of the framework. I highly recommend this to anyone wanting to build a school culture rooted in joy, responsibility, and connection.'

Guidance Officer, Department of Education, QLD

'Connecting with Bernii and her team has been an incredible experience! Bernii's extensive knowledge of Loving Our Students On

Purpose has given us a framework and language to begin transforming our school culture into one of belonging and connection. Bernii is an engaging and warm speaker who genuinely connects with the schools she works with.'

Nicole Hawkins – Senior Youth Worker, YMCA, Bundaberg, Australia

'Having never engaged in professional supervision before, I was unsure of the benefits. Bernii has a natural ability to challenge thought processes, fostering a growth mindset. At one point, I questioned my capacity to stay in my role. Bernii made time for an unscheduled session to unpack the challenges I was facing. The extra support recalibrated my focus, and I now thrive in my role. Thank you, Bernii!'

Matthew Gilbank – Teacher, Calvary Christian College, Townsville, Australia

'Our teachers were delighted by Bernii's Loving Our Students On Purpose workshop, one of the best they had attended. They were reminded how to maintain respect through regulating emotions and provided with simple but effective scripts to use in the classroom. We particularly appreciated learning about brain development and how we can support students through this period.'

Parent Testimony – Parkridge, Australia

'When I think back on the trauma of those school years, my time with Bernii and the principals were some of the brightest moments. They walked alongside us with hope and grace, calmly offering solutions while empowering us as parents. Bernii's love never wavered, and my boys, now in their twenties, express gratitude for her persistence, even during their most rebellious years.'